MARGARET MORGAN
and
MARY MORGAN PEDLOW

Memorial

RIVERSIDE   PUBLIC   LIBRARY

Exploring NORTH
AMERICA

Book Editor   April McCroskie

Designed and Produced by
The Salariya Book Company Ltd
Brighton, England.

Illustrated by   David Antram

Published by
PETER BEDRICK BOOKS
2112 Broadway
New York, NY 10023

Published in agreement with
Macdonald Young Books Ltd,
England

Library of Congress
Cataloging-in-Publication Data
Morley, Jacqueline.
  Exploring North America /
Jacqueline Morley : [illustrated by]
David Antram.
     p. cm.
Summary: Tells the story of how
Europeans got to know the size and
shape of the northern part of the
New World, an area discovered over
a period of four centuries.
   Includes index.
ISBN 0-87226-488-2
  1. North America – Discovery and
exploration – Juvenile literature.
[1. North America – Discovery and
exploration. 2. Explorers.]
I. Antram, David, 1958-   ill.
II. Title.
E45.M69   1996   96-1926
970.01 – dc20   CIP
                                       AC

Second printing, 1997

Printed in Hong Kong

Exploring NORTH AMERICA

Jacqueline Morley

David Antram

PETER BEDRICK BOOKS

NEW YORK

CONTENTS

For clarity, regions of America are referred to by their modern names. When they were discovered, they had no official names.

INTRODUCTION

You might think that Christopher Columbus discovered North America in 1492, but you would be wrong. The year 1492 is one of the most famous dates in world history and for Europeans it was a momentous year. It marked the beginning of their exploration of what came to be known as the New World. In that year Columbus landed on an island off the coast of Florida and thought that he had reached some part of Asia by sailing west from Spain. What he did not realize was that he had not gone nearly far enough, and that a vast continent lay between him and his goal. Though his explorations brought him close to America's huge land mass, the only points where he touched it briefly were in Central and South America. He gets the glory because his discoveries were the first to make European rulers aware of new lands in the west. But Columbus was not the first European to find these new lands; the Vikings had got there 500 years earlier.

We will leave aside the question of whether someone can claim to have "discovered" a land which already has inhabitants. This book tells the story of how Europeans got to know the size and shape of the northern part of the New World. Its explorers came from many nations and had many motives: patriotism, greed, ambition, restlessness and pure curiosity. And because the unknown area was so vast, its forests so deep, its plains so wide and its mountain barriers so forbidding, at least four centuries were needed to discover its secrets.

Early Explorers

In 1493 Christopher Columbus returned to Spain with amazing news – he thought he had succeeded in reaching Asia by sailing west. At this time, Asia was the source of precious trade goods like silks, spices and gems. European rulers wanted to make the most of this trade without depending on the eastern traders who brought the goods overland. It looked as though Spain had found a way of reaching these eastern markets directly, by sailing to them from the west.

Columbus's achievement has overshadowed other attempts. For example, John Cabot – an Italian like Columbus – had been planning a similar scheme for years. He finally persuaded England's King Henry VII to invest in a search for a northerly route to China, to compete with Spain.

In 1497 Cabot reached what was probably Newfoundland. (In fact the Vikings had hit a similar spot 500 years before). In 1498 Cabot made a second trip, but his ships vanished and no one knows what happened to him and his crew.

Cabot, like Columbus, was convinced that he had reached Asia but later voyagers soon cast doubt on this. By 1507 the new land had been given a name – America. On world maps its northern half appeared as an uncertain coastline linking Spain's Florida with the lands that Cabot had claimed on behalf of England – its vast hinterland was yet to be explored.

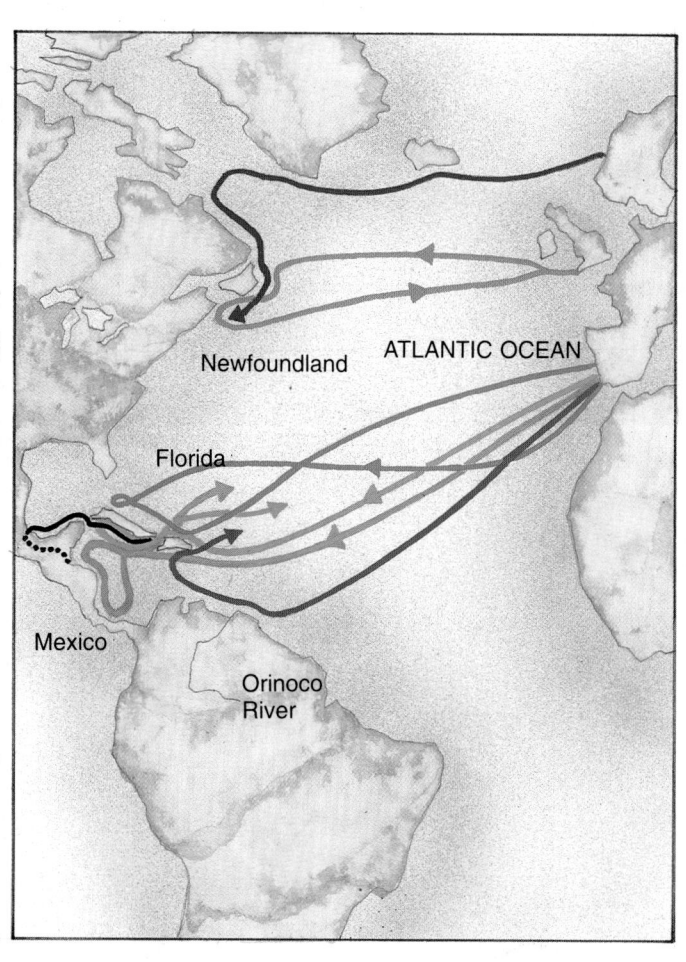

Newfoundland

ATLANTIC OCEAN

Florida

Mexico

Orinoco River

A 15TH-CENTURY COMPASS. At this time voyagers had only very simple instruments to guide them: a compass enabled them to judge the direction in which they were sailing, a quadrant helped to calculate latitude, but longitude had to be guessed at.

— Vikings c. AD 1000

Christopher Columbus:
First voyage 1492-3
Second voyage 1493-6
Third voyage 1498
Fourth voyage 1502-4

John Cabot 1497

— Hernan Cortés 1518-21
···· Hernan Cortés 1524-6

TOBER 1492. Columbus was
ost in tropical waters when he
e the first landfall in the
v World, in the Bahamas, to
south east of Florida.
ther south he found Cuba,
Hispaniola (modern Haiti
the Dominican Republic).

WHEN COLUMBUS SKIRTED the
mouth of the Orinoco River on
his third voyage he knew from
the river's tremendous flow
that it must come from a vast
continent. He wrote: "I have
reached the tip of Asia and I
have seen one of its great rivers".

COLUMBUS FOUND LITTLE
gold, but it was rumored that
on the mainland people lived in
cities of gold. Hernan Cortés
was sent from Spain to Mexico
to find these magnificent cities.

JUNE 1497. While Columbus
was still making his discoveries,
Cabot's ship, the *Matthew*, found
the shores of Newfoundland
more than 1,500 miles to the
north. He assumed it was a
remote part of Asia.

CABOT MET NO inhabitants
but found possessions which
suggested that they wore skins
rather than silks. He returned
without Asia's riches, but he told
of seas so full of cod that they
could be scooped up in baskets.

**The *Matthew*
reaches Newfoundland.**

7

Treasure Seekers

The gold that Cortés found in Mexico encouraged the rulers of Spain to look for more in the surrounding lands. In 1528 Pánfilo de Narváez, the governor of Mexico, was given the right to conquer and colonize land between Florida and eastern Mexico. He landed on the Florida coast with 400 men. Despite being warned by a companion, Alvar Núñez Cabeza de Vaca, that it would be unwise to lose contact with his fleet, he sent it off along the coast while he led the main party inland. He did not find the great cities he was looking for, only scattered villages where people, by Spanish standards, lived in poverty. They were hostile, which was not surprising, since the Spaniards soon ran out of food and began to take theirs. Narváez was an incompetent leader. After weeks of wandering around, he had little idea where he was and could not find his fleet. Stranded on the coast with no food, his group of starving men decided to build boats even though no one knew how to. Five "homemade" boats eventually set sail but were soon scattered. Three boats – including the one Narváez was sailing in – disappeared for good.

IN 1513 Juan Ponce de León's vessel skirted the mangrove swamps of the Florida coast. Ponce de León had found gold in Puerto Rico and hoped that land to the north held more.

THE SPANISH BELIEVED in many legends, like that of El Dorado, a king covered in gold. Ponce de León was lookin for the Fountain of Youth when he discovered Florida.

JUAN PONCE DE LEÓN, a Spanish nobleman, discovered Florida. He explored its Atlantic coastline, then doubled back around its tip and along the Gulf shore.

Gila River

ATLANTIC OCEAN

MEXICO

GULF OF MEXICO

Florida

Mexico City •

CUBA

HISPANIOLA

PUERTO RICO

Ponce de León 1513

Narváez 1527-8

Cabeza de Vaca 1527-36

Father Marcos and Esteban 1539

THE SPANISH set off armed with weapons like this Spanish soldier's helmet and matchlock musket. They did this as a precaution and because they wanted to conquer and subdue the native people. Their guns terrified the natives and their horses astonished them – horses were unknown in America then.

CABEZA DE VACA and his companions wandered through the deserts of Texas and New Mexico. They became traders, but the people they met were mostly poor hunter-gatherers with little to trade. Some thought that the four strangers must have magic powers and asked them to heal the sick. Esteban, the black member of the group, went exploring again. In 1539 he was one of a group led by a Franciscan friar, Marcos de Niza. They went further north beyond the Gila River in Arizona.

The four men struggling through the desert.

There were 15 survivors from the Narváez expedition but we know what happened to only four of them, one of whom was Cabeza de Vaca. They reached the mainland and were kept captive by Yaqui tribesmen for 5 years, then wandered 1,200 miles on foot to the Gulf of California, finally reaching safety at the Spanish settlement of Mexico City in 1536.

Conquistadores

The lure of gold brought a rush of Spanish adventurers to the New World. In the 1530s vast riches had been found amongst the Inca people of Peru. The Spaniards thought the north would be full of treasure, too. Spain authorized military expeditions led by commanders known as conquistadores to claim land for Spain. The Spanish government expected the conquistadores to treat the local people well – unless they refused to become Christians and Spanish subjects. But the government could not control the conquistadores' actions, which were ruled by greed. One of the most ruthless was Hernando de Soto who took over the conquest of Florida after Narváez's disastrous attempt. He landed in 1539 and began a brutal search for gold, torturing and killing natives because he thought they were refusing to tell him where to find it.

De Soto's quest took him north through Georgia and South Carolina. He then went westward over the Appalachian Mountains and across Alabama, where he had a bloody battle with Creek Indians. Many of his troops were killed.

IN MAY 1539 de Soto's party landed in Florida and prepared to set up camp. De Soto brought at least 600 men, 200 horses and a large pack of dogs. He had a herd of pigs for food, too.

SEVERAL PRIESTS accompanied the expedition. Though they were tough, the conquistadores were devout Catholics who wanted to hear mass regularly and convert the heathen natives.

By 1541 de Soto's party had reached the Mississippi. They were the first Europeans to stand on the banks of this mighty river. They crossed it and continued west in hope of reaching the Pacific, but the land was so barren that they were forced to turn back. In 1542, close to the Mississippi, de Soto died of fever.

THE EUROPEANS expected the native people to feed them. If they were hostile, their villages were plundered and they were taken prisoner. They were put in iron collars and chains and forced to carry the supplies.

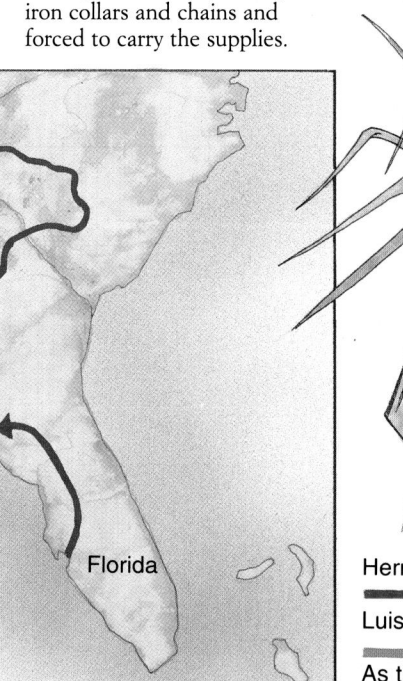

Mississippi River

Florida

GULF OF MEXICO

MEXICO

Hernando de Soto 1539-42

Luis de Moscoso 1542-3

As the routes are based on an account published 63 years later, they are not exact.

Conquistadores' expedition.

PEOPLE who refused to cooperate with the invaders were put to the sword, burned alive, or thrown to the pack of fierce dogs that accompanied the Spaniards everywhere.

542, DE SOTO, the discoverer f the Mississippi was buried in ts waters. (The Spanish named he river the *Espiritu Santo*, neaning Holy Spirit). Luis de Moscoso took command and ried to reach the Spanish ettlement in Mexico. Again tarvation forced the expedition ack. Moscoso ordered his men o build boats (luckily one man vas a sailor) and they managed o reach the mouth of the Mississippi and sail to Mexico.

The Grand Canyon

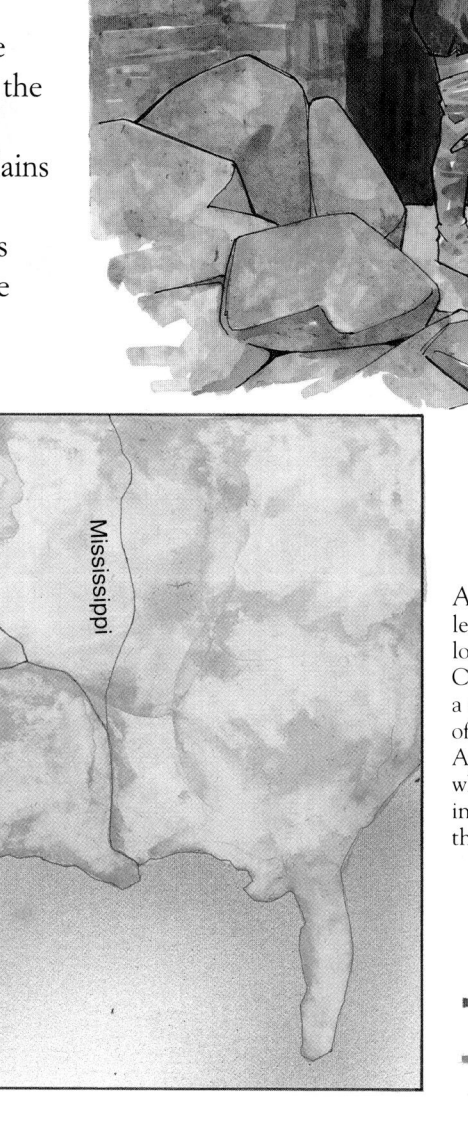

The Spaniards would not give up hope of finding gold in North America. When Father Marcos returned from his travels (*see page 9*) with stories of Zuñi Indians with houses several stories high, his tales were seized upon as proof that one of the legendary "Seven Golden Cities of Cibola" had at last been found. The next year, an expedition under Francisco Vásquez de Coronado set off to find these cities of fabulous riches.

When Coronado reached the Indian settlement he must have been bitterly disappointed. The Indians were hostile – they had killed Esteban the previous year. There was a battle and the settlement was destroyed. Then Coronado turned his search eastward. He led his men across the Rio Grande river, through Texas, where they saw buffalo for the first time, across Oklahoma and onto the vast plains of Kansas. The immensity of the Great Plains astounded the Spaniards. "The country is like a bowl" Coronado wrote, "so that when a man sits down the horizon surrounds him all round at the distance of a musket shot."

A GROUP of Coronado's men, led by García López de Cárdenas, looked in wonder at the Grand Canyon with its drop of nearly a mile. They could see the waters of the Colorado River below. Apart from a missionary priest who rode by its edge on a mule in 1776, no European reached the canyon again until 1857.

Coronado 1540-42

Cárdenas 1540

Coronado's men at the Grand Canyon.

Before he set off east, after fighting with the Zuñis, Coronado had sent a scouting party west into Arizona, where it stumbled upon the Grand Canyon. Despite his expedition's amazing geographical discoveries, the Spanish government considered it a failure and Coronado met a cool reception for returning to Spain without gold.

A 16TH-CENTURY PORTRAIT of a buffalo. Coronado said they had beards like large she-goats, and bulging eyes, so that when they ran they could see who followed them.

ON THE GREAT PLAINS Coronado and his men saw the nomadic Plains Indians who followed the huge herds of buffalo. He noted how their way of life depended on them.

13

The Western Sea

Spain's wealth and possessions in the New World became the envy of Europe. Nations like the French, English and Dutch were determined to discover something to their advantage in these lands. Since Spain controlled the Caribbean area, it was clearly sensible to look further north. With this in mind, Francis I of France commissioned an Italian navigator, Giovanni da Verrazano, to explore the coast north of Florida. If a navigable strait could be found it would be possible to sail much further west and perhaps find a direct sea route to China. No one had any idea yet of the true breadth of the continent; the Atlantic shore might fringe a narrow strip of land or a group of close-set islands, so the French strategy seemed sensible.

Verrazano set off in 1524, reaching the American coast in the area of North Carolina. He sailed north, exploring the coastline as far as Newfoundland. Somewhere along the way – it is not clear where, but perhaps near Pamlico Sound in North Carolina – he saw what he thought was the sea, separated from the Atlantic by a belt of land. The knowledge that the king was hoping for just such a find probably influenced Verrazano's impression. Reports of this "western sea" were eagerly received in Europe. When people settled on the Atlantic coast in the 17th century they realized that this inland sea must be some way off, but the idea of its existence, somewhere just beyond the known horizon, beckoned to explorers for centuries.

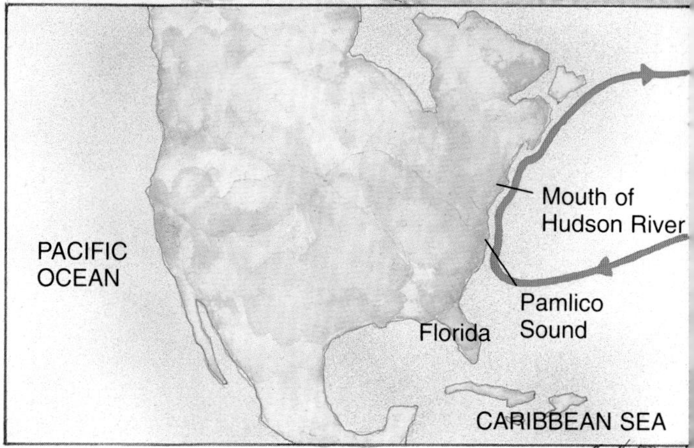

PACIFIC OCEAN

Mouth of Hudson River

Florida

Pamlico Sound

CARIBBEAN SEA

Verrazano's route, 1524.

The king provided Verrazano with the *Dauphine*, a French naval vessel. He sailed in this from Madeira.

FROM THE MASTHEAD of the *Dauphine*, (*right*), an excited look-out called to the crew below. There was water in the distance stretching as far as the eye could see.

GEOGRAPHERS were delighted with Verrazano's news. It confirmed what they believed must be true. Some maps, like this one (*below*), transformed his isthmus into a strait.

A BUST OF GIOVANNI DA VERRAZANO. Though his western sea was a fantasy, Verrazano has genuine discoveries to his credit. On April 17, 1524, he found the mouth of the Hudson River and anchored in what is now the entrance to New York Harbor. He described it as "a very pleasant place, situated among certain steep little hills. There ran down into the sea a great stream of water, which within the mouth was very deep. Any great vessel might pass up."

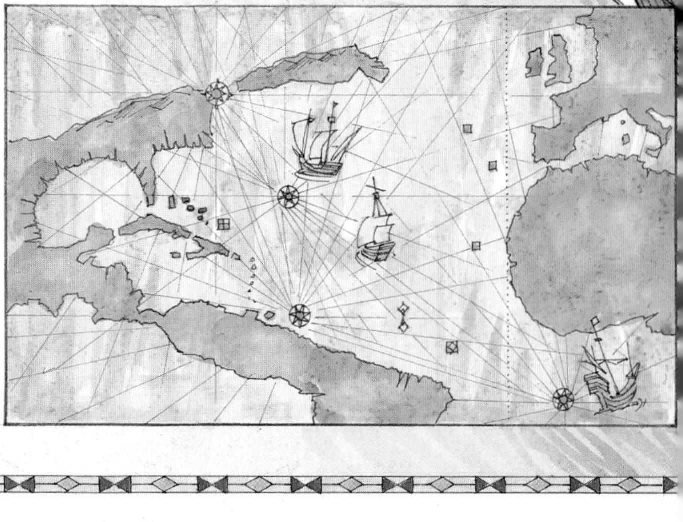

VERRAZANO MUST HAVE been misled by a long wide sandspit, with vegetation, which had formed across the mouth of the bay. He was too wary of the local inhabitants to land and investigate.

Verrazano thinks he has found the western sea.

A QUADRANT was used to navigate. The straight edge had two sights which had to be aligned with the sun or a certain star. The point where the plumbline then fell across the curved edge, which was marked with a scale, told the sailors their latitude.

The Northwest Passage

The precious strait that would lead to China was not to be found where Verrazano had hoped, but why should it not lie farther north? The nation that could find it and control access to it would have an enormous trading advantage. Several rulers were prepared to finance such an exploration in the hope of long-term gain.

The French sent Jacques Cartier in the 1530s. He thought he might have found a strait, but it proved to be the Saint Lawrence estuary. He sailed up river and established the French claim to Canada. Martin Frobisher, an Englishman, was looking for an even more northerly route (what became known as the northwest passage) when he sailed past the southern tip of Greenland and reached Baffin Island in 1576. In 1609 the Dutch sent English navigator, Henry Hudson, to find a northeast passage to China by sailing north of Russia. The way was blocked by ice, so he went west to the New World. He rediscovered the Hudson estuary, claiming the region for Holland, and went far enough up the river to realize that this was not the way to China. The following year he tried again on England's behalf.

Cartier 1534	——
Cartier 1535-6	——
Frobisher 1576	——
Hudson 1609	——
Hudson 1610-11	——

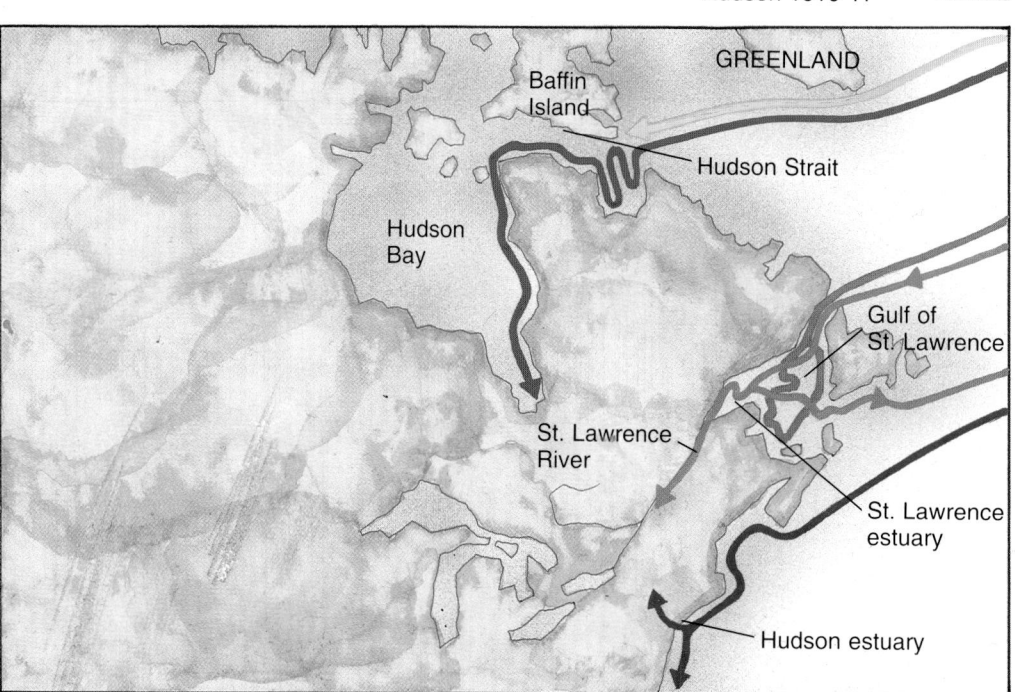

GREENLAND

Baffin Island

Hudson Strait

Hudson Bay

St. Lawrence River

Gulf of St. Lawrence

St. Lawrence estuary

Hudson estuary

A skirmish on Baffin Island.

LA GRANDE HERMINE, (1535) was the ship that Cartier sailed in on the second of his three trips to the New World. He went up the Saint Lawrence estuary, as far as present-day Montreal, but failed to start a settlement.

Like Frobisher, Hudson kept clear of the region the French had claimed and tried the far north, sailing through the Hudson Strait into what seemed to be a huge sea, now known as Hudson Bay. His ship was icebound and had to stay the winter, but when the ice melted his crew mutinied and abandoned him.

1611 (*below*). After a terrible winter, Hudson's crew refused to explore his new "sea" any further. They set him adrift in a boat with eight crew members (including his son), and sailed for home. No one knows what happened to the castaways.

IN 1576 Frobisher and his men had a few skirmishes with the people of Baffin Island. The boat scene was recorded by an artist who went on Frobisher's second trip. Frobisher mistook a 50 mile inlet for the strait he was seeking.

INUIT WOMAN (*left*) of Baffin Island with her child in her hood. The facial features of the Inuit convinced Frobisher that he had reached Asia.

17

Champdain

While their rulers longed for North American gold or a quick route to the east, ordinary people had been making modest fortunes across the north Atlantic. Within a few years of Cabot's discovery of Newfoundland in 1497, French, Portuguese, Basque and British boats were visiting its waters for easy and profitable catches of fish. Even before Cartier got there, fishing vessels had explored the northeast coast and the Gulf of Saint Lawrence. By the 1600s, trade was bringing increasing numbers of adventurous people to the area. They set up trading stations, and brought back cod, whale oil and, most profitable of all, beaver furs which they obtained from the native people.

In 1608 Samuel de Champlain, a Frenchman who had experience of trading in the area, arrived with a force of people to set up a permanent colony. On the Saint Lawrence River he built a fort which developed into a great fur-trading center (now Quebec). The following year he discovered a lake which he named Lake Champlain. Later he explored the Ottawa River and reached Lake Huron. In 1615 he discovered Lake Ontario.

Champlain made friends with the local Huron and Algonquin people. Sadly, this had unforeseen results. His men, armed with guns, supported them in raids against the Iroquois. This made the Iroquois bitter enemies of the French. It also taught the Native Americans to want guns, and this made tribal warfare much more deadly in later years.

IN 1615 CHAMPLAIN kept the promise he had made to his Huron allies: to support them in a campaign against the Iroquois. Together they besieged an Iroquois fort. The fort had a palisade (fence) 30 feet high and was protected on three sides by a lake and streams.

CHAMPLAIN INSTRUCTED the Hurons to build a moveable tower from which they could fire at the Iroquois. He also got them to make wooden screens to protect themselves against arrows. They hid behind these screens and crept up to the fort so they could set fire to its walls.

1609, (below). While Champlain was accompanying a fighting expedition of Algonquins and Hurons, he came across a beautiful lake, which he named after himself.

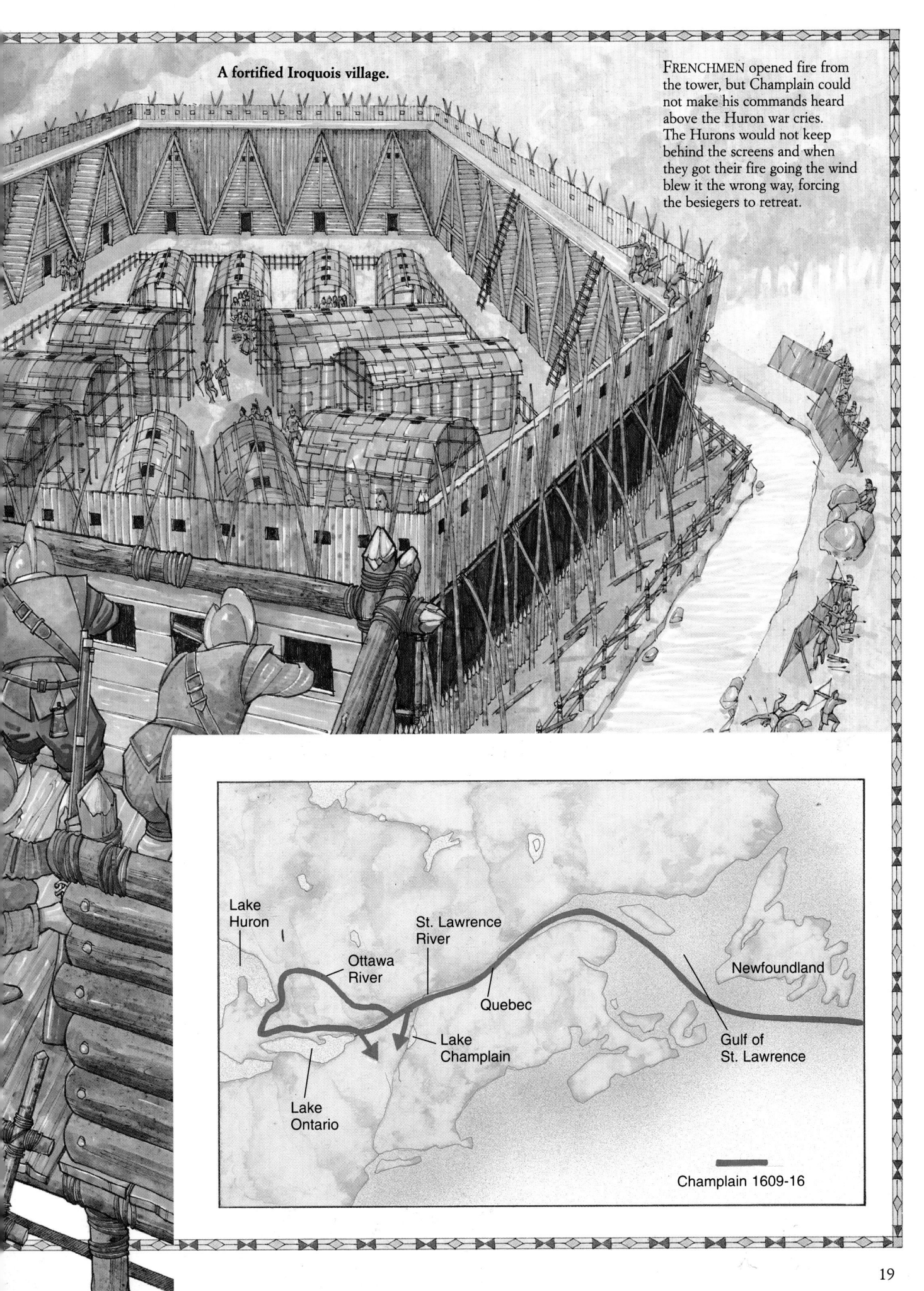

A fortified Iroquois village.

FRENCHMEN opened fire from the tower, but Champlain could not make his commands heard above the Huron war cries. The Hurons would not keep behind the screens and when they got their fire going the wind blew it the wrong way, forcing the besiegers to retreat.

Lake Huron

Ottawa River

St. Lawrence River

Newfoundland

Quebec

Lake Champlain

Gulf of St. Lawrence

Lake Ontario

Champlain 1609-16

Building a Canoe

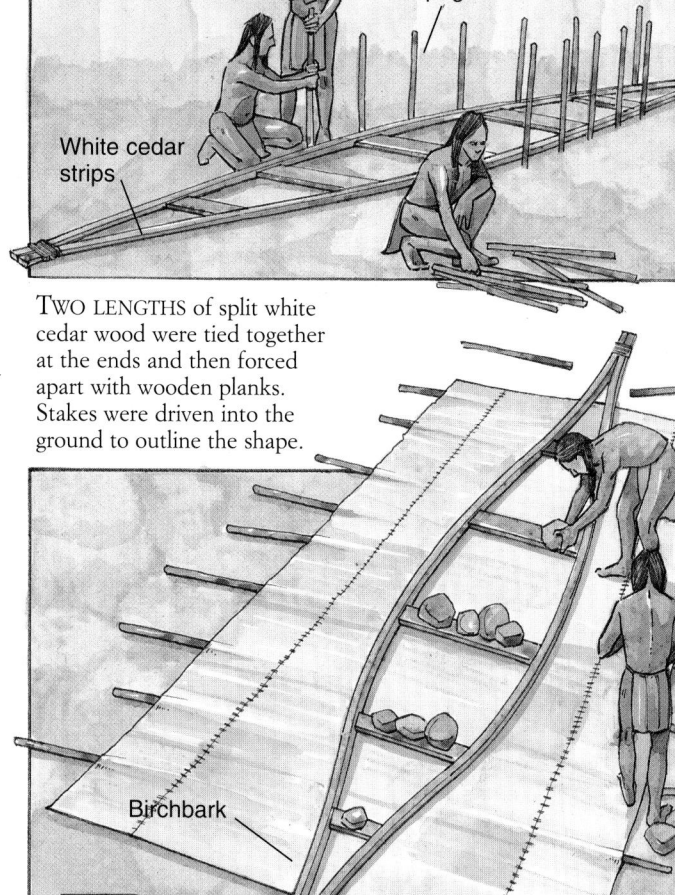

Champlain believed in trying to understand and learn from local people. It was from them that he heard of the existence of the Great Lakes, long before he saw them. They also told him of a giant waterfall (Niagara) that blocked travel by water beyond the head of Lake Ontario. Champlain often went on long journeys with his Huron or Algonquin allies, alone or with just a couple of French companions. He saw that the best way of getting around this vast land was to do as local people did. He encouraged his men to use canoes, which was a strange idea to them at first.

Champlain spent 20 years of his life establishing the French colony in Canada (New France) and encouraging its fur trade. Much of this time was taken up with administration and he had to send out agents to explore regions that he would have liked to visit himself. He trained an 18-year-old called Etienne Brûlé to be an interpreter and explorer by sending him to live for a year with a Native American tribe. At the end of the year Brûlé was so much one of them that he spent most of the rest of his life living with the Hurons. He roamed throughout the Great Lakes area and may have been the first white person to see many places that were "discovered" later. Brûlé was with Champlain when he found Lake Huron and Lake Ontario. It was probably Brûlé who discovered Lake Superior, but he left no written accounts so we cannot be sure.

Upright markers

White cedar strips

TWO LENGTHS of split white cedar wood were tied together at the ends and then forced apart with wooden planks. Stakes were driven into the ground to outline the shape.

Birchbark

THE FRAME was removed and then the stakes were laid flat and covered with sheets of birchbark. After this, the frame was placed on the sheets and weighted down with stones.

THE BARK was bent up round the frame. As this was done, the stakes were pounded into their holes to hold the bark in place. Battens were lashed to them to hold the sides firm.

IF A STRONG CURRENT made paddling impossible, Canadian traders used poles to punt their loaded canoes upstream. In very deep water they towed them with ropes.

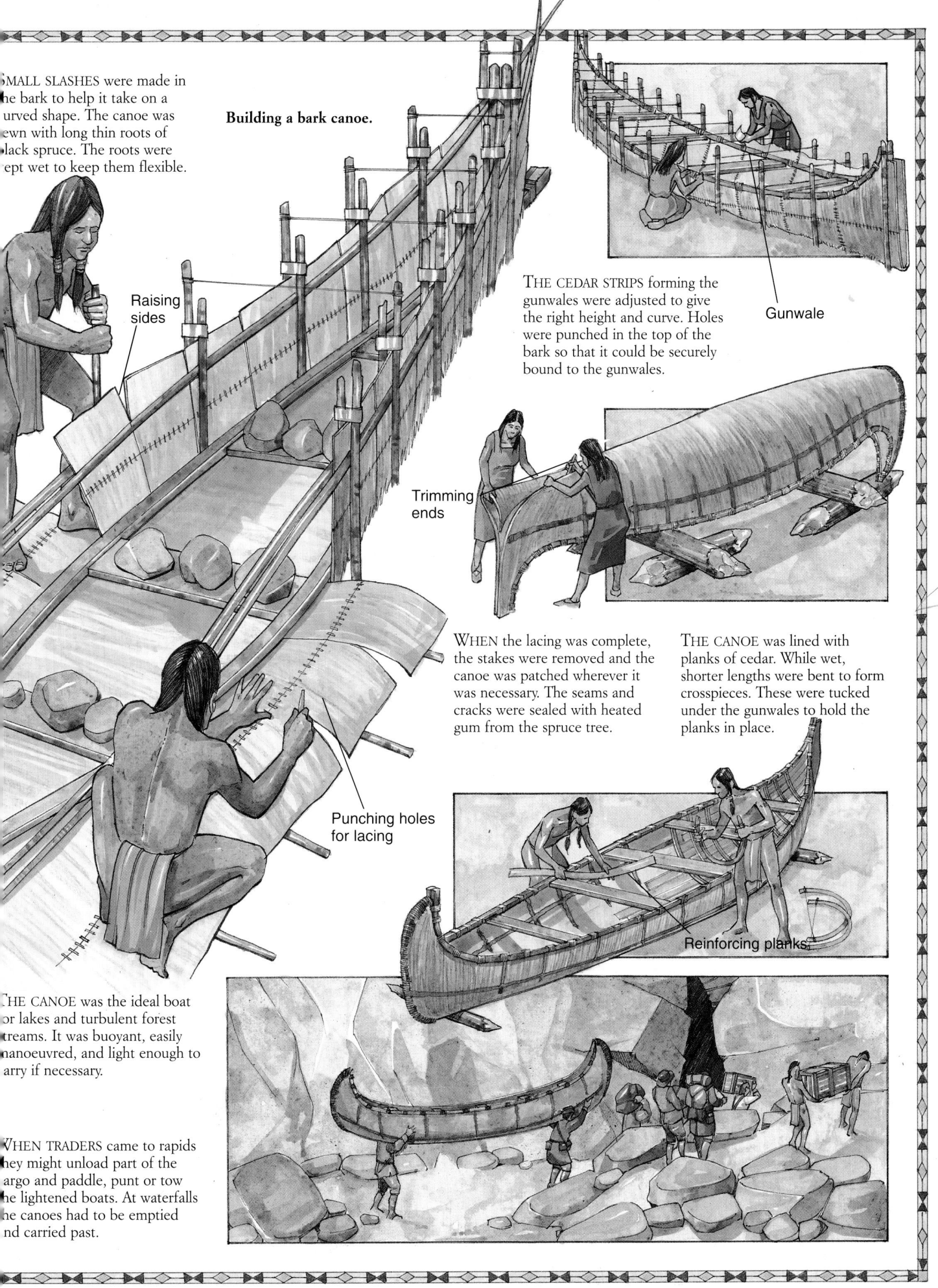

SMALL SLASHES were made in the bark to help it take on a curved shape. The canoe was sewn with long thin roots of black spruce. The roots were kept wet to keep them flexible.

Building a bark canoe.

Raising sides

Punching holes for lacing

THE CANOE was the ideal boat for lakes and turbulent forest streams. It was buoyant, easily manoeuvred, and light enough to carry if necessary.

WHEN TRADERS came to rapids they might unload part of the cargo and paddle, punt or tow the lightened boats. At waterfalls the canoes had to be emptied and carried past.

THE CEDAR STRIPS forming the gunwales were adjusted to give the right height and curve. Holes were punched in the top of the bark so that it could be securely bound to the gunwales.

Gunwale

Trimming ends

WHEN the lacing was complete, the stakes were removed and the canoe was patched wherever it was necessary. The seams and cracks were sealed with heated gum from the spruce tree.

THE CANOE was lined with planks of cedar. While wet, shorter lengths were bent to form crosspieces. These were tucked under the gunwales to hold the planks in place.

Reinforcing planks

Coureurs de Bois

Though Champlain was a practical man he had, like all great explorers, a vivid imagination. He longed to discover the "western sea" that led to China. On first hearing Native American accounts of the huge inland seas beyond the Saint Lawrence, he assured the French king that "the means of reaching the kingdom of China and the East Indies" was now within his grasp. When Champlain saw these "seas" (the Great Lakes), though magnificent, they were disappointingly not the "western sea". But perhaps they might lead there? In 1634 he sent one of his agents, Jean Nicolet, to find out. Nicolet traveled by boat across Lake Huron, far beyond the point that Champlain had reached. Then he crossed Lake Michigan and landed on its western shore.

Nicolet had brought with him a long robe of Chinese damask embroidered with flowers and birds. There was still a belief that North America could be a peninsula (strip of land) attached to Asia, so he thought it would be appropriate to wear the robe when he met the inhabitants of this far-off land. He amazed the Winnebago Indians who greeted him on the shore: they thought he was a god.

The Winnebagoes told Nicolet that some way further to the west a great river flowed. They called it the Mississippi. Nicolet had come so far west already, he felt sure that this river must be the great waterway that, according to geographers' optimistic statements, flowed through the continent into the western sea.

Nicolet astounds the Winnebago Indians.

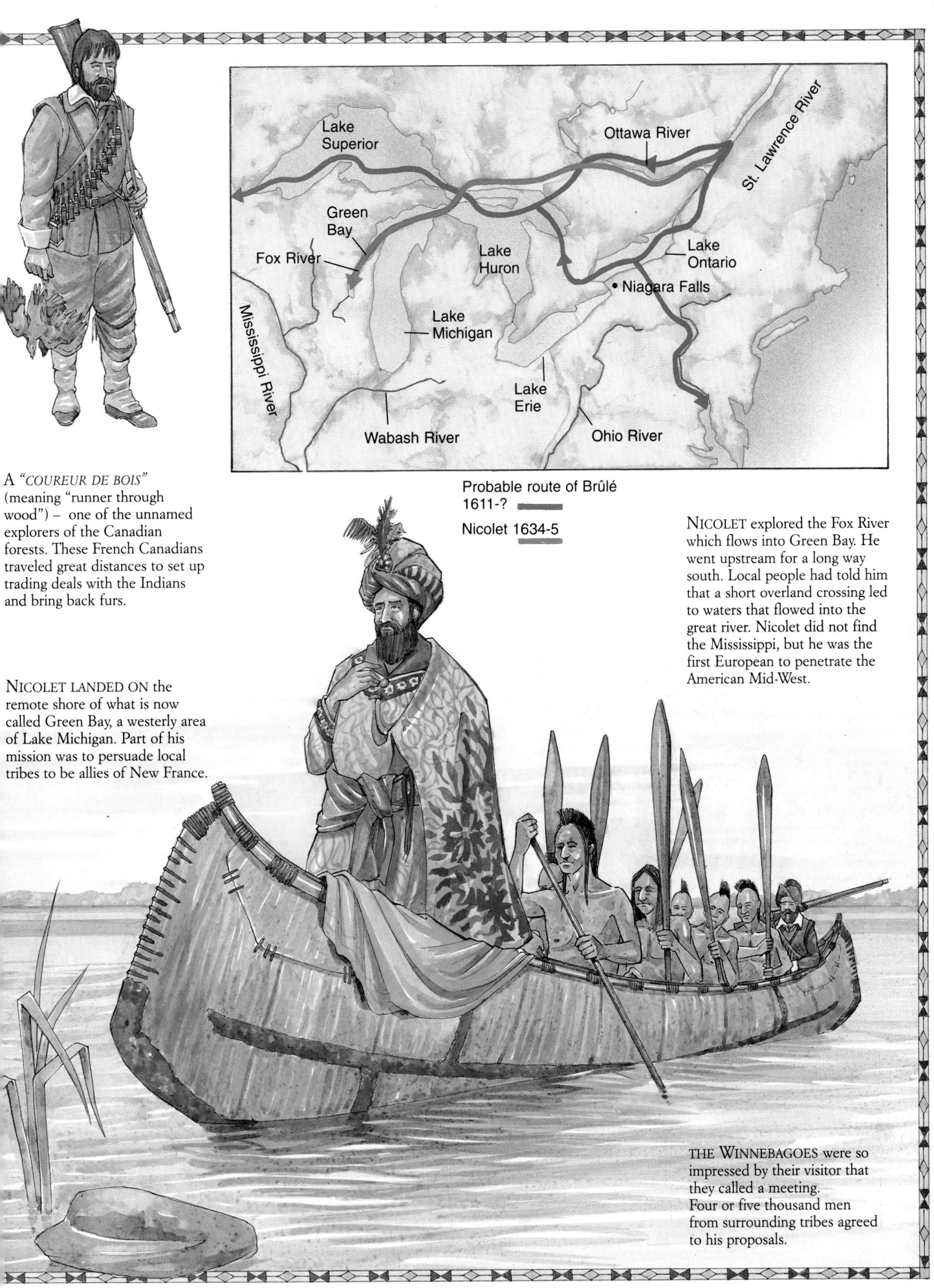

Lake Superior

Ottawa River

St. Lawrence River

Green Bay

Fox River

Lake Huron

Lake Ontario

• Niagara Falls

Mississippi River

Lake Michigan

Lake Erie

Wabash River

Ohio River

Probable route of Brûlé 1611-?

Nicolet 1634-5

A *"COUREUR DE BOIS"* (meaning "runner through wood") – one of the unnamed explorers of the Canadian forests. These French Canadians traveled great distances to set up trading deals with the Indians and bring back furs.

NICOLET LANDED ON the remote shore of what is now called Green Bay, a westerly area of Lake Michigan. Part of his mission was to persuade local tribes to be allies of New France.

NICOLET explored the Fox River which flows into Green Bay. He went upstream for a long way south. Local people had told him that a short overland crossing led to waters that flowed into the great river. Nicolet did not find the Mississippi, but he was the first European to penetrate the American Mid-West.

THE WINNEBAGOES were so impressed by their visitor that they called a meeting. Four or five thousand men from surrounding tribes agreed to his proposals.

Missionaries

The first Roman Catholic missionaries arrived in New France in 1615, to convert the Huron and Algonquin Indians to the Catholic faith. By the 1630s many missionaries, mostly Jesuits, were doing mission work in the Canadian forests. In order to explain Christianity clearly, they set about learning Native American languages and living among the Native Americans to understand their customs. "You must visit them in their cabins oftener than once a day, if you would perform your duty as you ought" one wrote. They traveled courageously into the wilds to carry the Christian message as far as their strength would allow. In the process they discovered new routes and visited places where no Europeans had been before.

AS THEY GOT to the point where the waters of the Missouri, white with mud, swept into the Mississippi, Joliet and Father Marquette urged their crews to steer the two fragile canoes to the eastern bank. This was so that they could keep clear of all the dead trees and broken branches that floated in the Missouri River's current.

One of the most famous missionary explorers was Father Jacques Marquette. In 1673 he joined a fur trader, Louis Joliet, in an epic journey down the "great river". The French had learned of it from Nicolet but had not seen it. Joliet's mission was to find the western sea. When at last they reached the Mississippi they found it carried them not west, but south. They were swept past the mouths of two huge tributaries (the Missouri and the Ohio), and were far down into Arkansas when the local people told them of white traders to the south. These could only be the Spanish. The explorers then realised that their Mississippi was in fact Spain's *Espiritu Santo* and that it would not flow into the western sea. Fearful of the hostile Spaniards, they turned back.

Descending the Mississippi.

A BRAVE JESUIT missionary greets a group of Iroquois warriors. Though the Iroquois were hostile to the French and their religion, many Hurons were converted.

THE MISSIONARIES often went alone and unarmed into unknown territory. In 1665 Father Allouez went in a canoe around Lake Superior and north to Lake Nipigon.

THE JESUITS built a mission headquarters, deep in Huron territory, which was known as Sainte Marie among the Hurons. It had to be fortified to protect it from the Iroquois.

THE JESUITS raised a cross outside the chapel of their new mission village. The priests themselves destroyed the mission in 1649 to stop it falling into the hands of the Iroquois.

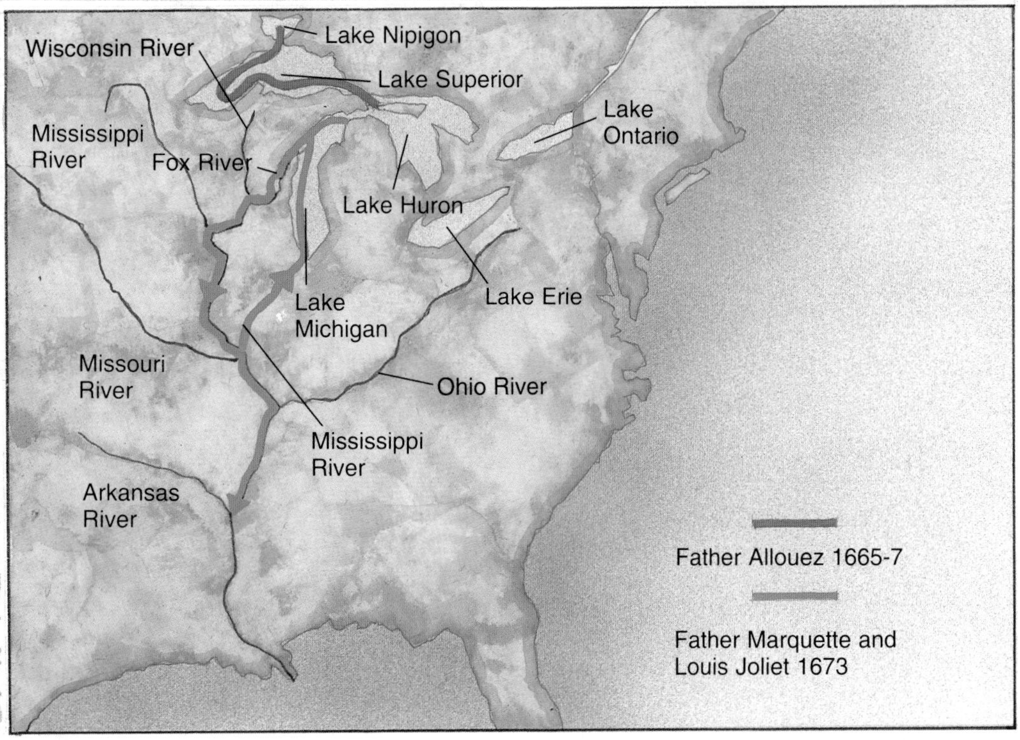

Wisconsin River — Lake Nipigon

— Lake Superior

Mississippi River

Fox River

Lake Ontario

Lake Huron

Lake Michigan

Lake Erie

Missouri River

Ohio River

Mississippi River

Arkansas River

Father Allouez 1665-7

Father Marquette and Louis Joliet 1673

Niagara Falls

The French now realized that they had not found the key to the west. The Mississippi did not flow to the Pacific, but to the Gulf of Mexico. This news inspired a French military engineer, Robert Cavelier de la Salle, to propose a giant enterprise – the building of a string of trading forts from the Great Lakes to the mouth of the Mississippi. This would enable the French to export furs via the Gulf as well as the Saint Lawrence, and to cut off the Spanish in Florida from those in Mexico.

La Salle began his project in 1678, starting west via Lake Ontario to Lake Erie. His party of 30 included an eccentric French priest named Father Louis Hennepin. They had to carry their boats and equipment around Niagara Falls which blocked the passage of boats between the lakes. Above Niagara, La Salle built his first fort and a ship, the *Griffon*, to sail on the lakes.

Hennepin later wrote several best-selling books about his travels. He published a spectacular print of the Falls and managed to give the impression that he had discovered them. In fact, he made himself a member of expeditions he had not even been on. But he did have at least one major discovery to his credit. La Salle sent him north to set up trading posts on the upper Mississippi. He was captured by the Sioux Indians, who took him to their tribal grounds in distant Minnesota. There, in 1680 near modern Minneapolis, Hennepin saw and named the Saint Anthony Falls.

LA SALLE and his men were stunned at the spectacle of Niagara. Though the Falls had been known of from Native American reports for over 50 years, their very existence had deterred traders from using this route. The name of the first European to see them is unknown.

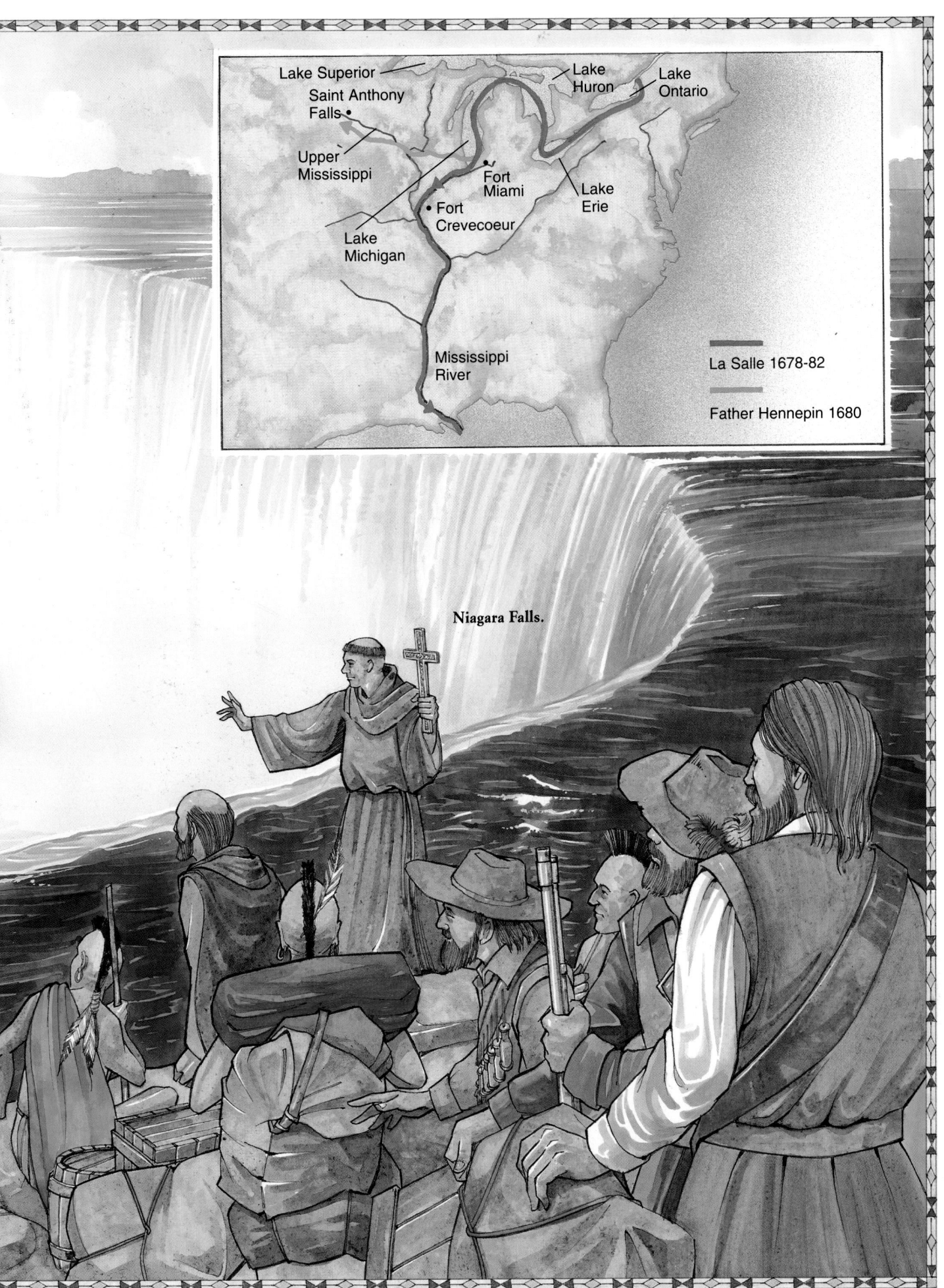

Lake Superior

Saint Anthony Falls •

Upper Mississippi

Lake Michigan

Fort Crevecoeur •

• Fort Miami

Lake Huron

Lake Ontario

Lake Erie

Mississippi River

La Salle 1678-82

Father Hennepin 1680

Niagara Falls.

Louisiana

La Salle sailed the Great Lakes in the *Griffon*, collecting a shipload of furs to finance his Mississippi venture. He sent the ship back east in 1680, while he established another fort in the wilderness on the Illinois River and waited for supplies. Unknown to him, the *Griffon* and its precious furs had disappeared and were never seen again. La Salle was forced to make a journey back east on foot, in dreadful winter conditions, to raise the money to continue. Though heavily in debt, he managed to get financial support, but back at the fort he found that most of his men had deserted. La Salle named the fort "*Crevecoeur*" (heartbreak).

La Salle was determined not to admit defeat, and organized a new expedition which started down the Mississippi in January 1682. His descent of the river seemed a triumph and the tribes he met welcomed him. By April 1682 he stood on the shore of the Mexican Gulf and claimed for France all the land he had come through. In honor of the king, whose realm in New France he had doubled in size, he called the new territory Louisiana.

When La Salle returned to France he found that no one was impressed. "*Fort Inutile*" (useless) was Louis XIV's verdict on La Salle's achievement. Sailing back to the Gulf in 1684 to start a colony, La Salle overshot the mouth of the Mississippi by hundreds of miles (there was still no means of measuring longitude). He tried to find the river overland but was murdered by his rebellious men.

THE ALLIGATOR-INFESTED swamps of the Mississippi delta were very different from the northern forests that La Salle and his men had set off from. All of this vast area was claimed for France. In a ceremony on the shore, La Salle, dressed in coat of scarlet and gold, proclaimed the existence of Louisiana to the sound of musket shots and the singing of a solemn hymn.

APART FROM the river itself, Louisiana's interior was practically unknown. British colonists on the Atlantic had not yet crossed the coastal mountains, so nothing was known of the land between those and the Mississippi, nor of the land west of the river.

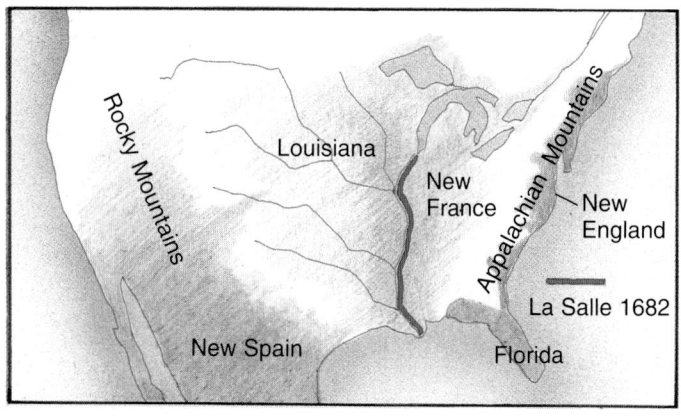

Rocky Mountains

Louisiana

New France

Appalachian Mountains

New England

La Salle 1682

New Spain

Florida

La Salle proclaims the existence of Louisiana.

MARCH 19,1687 (*below*), the death of La Salle. He set up his last fort close to the point where he had landed on the Texas coast. From there he tried several times to find the Mississippi River by trekking inland to the northeast. He was not a popular leader and somewhere in the wilds of Texas his men shot him.

The High Mountains

The way west remained a mystery in the 18th century. The secret had to lie in finding some great waterway cutting through the wilderness. Fur trader Pierre Gaultier de la Vérendrye thought he had the answer. He had learned from a Native American called Ochagach that a string of lakes lay somewhere west of Lake Superior. Full of hope, he set off in 1731. After five years of misfortunes he reached Lake Winnipeg. The lakes proved to stretch not west, but north, and emptied into Hudson Bay.

In October 1738 La Vérendrye set off from his fort near Lake Winnipeg on another quest: to follow a Native American trail across the prairie, deep into North Dakota. He went on foot, with two of his sons and some local Native American guides, to find Mandan Indians who were said to live on the banks of the distant Missouri River. The Mandans welcomed them, but questions about the way west had to be made in sign language and the answers were mystifying. Freezing weather forced the party back to the fort. By the time they reached it the following February, La Vérendrye was seriously ill.

A MAP OF "Western Canada", published in 1764, claimed to show recent discoveries. It shows a range of mountains just beyond the "western sea". Ochagach's map, which was given credit for the discoveries, is reproduced along the top edge.

La Vérendrye's sons went on with the search. In 1742 they went to consult horseriding tribes said to live in the far southwest. It was so far away that their guides deserted them. No one knows exactly where the brothers were when they saw high mountains stretching across the west.

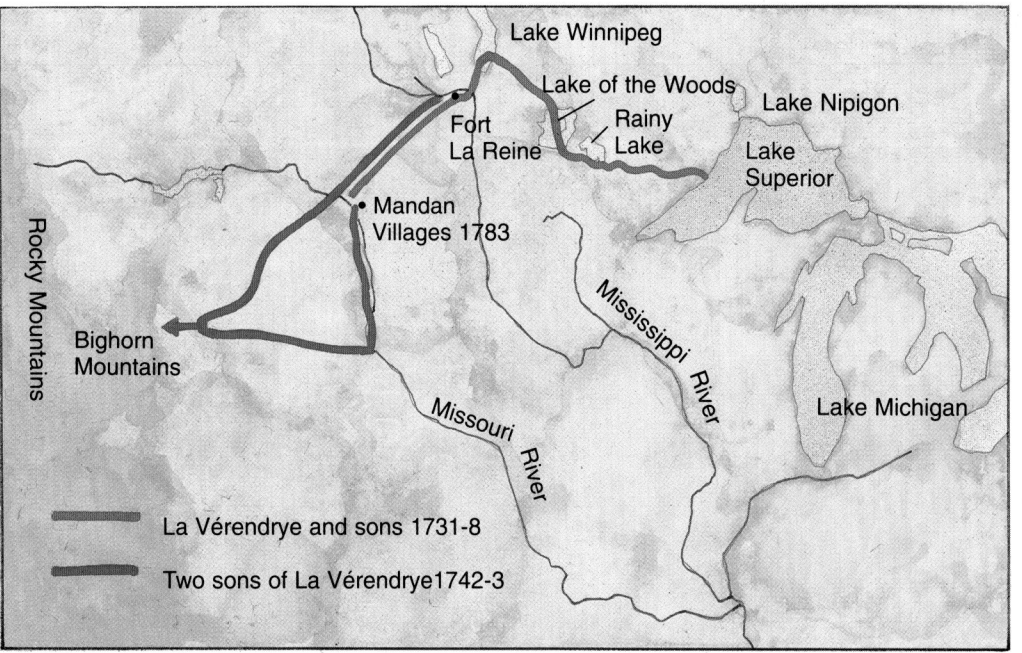

La Vérendrye and sons 1731-8

Two sons of La Vérendrye 1742-3

LA VÉRENDRYE met Ochagach at a fur-trading post near Lake Superior. Ochagach described a lake far to the west from which a westward-flowing river led to an even bigger "sea". La Vérendrye persuaded the Native American to draw a map on birchbark. Unfortunately it was far from accurate.

THE MAP (*left*) shows the probable route that La Vérendrye's sons took across the Great Plains. Even before the brothers' journey people knew that huge mountains lay somewhere to the west. Many Indian tribes had tales about them. Some described them as the Mountains of Shining Stones

THE "HORSE INDIANS" could not show La Vérendrye's sons the way to the sea, but they took them on a raiding expedition far over the prairies into Wyoming, to the foot of a mountain range.

THE BROTHERS were the first explorers to see the peaks that barred the way west. These may have been the main range of Rockies, or more likely the Bighorn Mountains.

Ochagach points the way to La Vérendrye.

Coast to Coast

WESTCOAST-INDIAN basket and ceremonial rattle. The Pacific peoples Mackenzie met had different lifestyles from those of the Canadian prairies.

After French Canada became British in 1763, British companies took over the fur trade. By the late 1770s traders had explored plains as far west as Lake Athabasca in Alberta. Then came the news that the British navigator, Captain Cook, had discovered a large inlet as he was sailing along the north Pacific coast. He had not actually seen a river, but optimists assumed this must be the western end of the great waterway that explorers had been looking for. Also Cook's men had bought furs from local Native Americans and sold them at vast profit in China. Companies based in Canada wanted a share of this trade but had no way of getting to it. Alexander Mackenzie, a Scottish company employee, set off from Lake Athabasca in 1789 to find one.

Mackenzie's first attempt ended in bitter disappointment. He found a westward-flowing river (now named after him), but it bent north as it neared the mountains and carried him to the Arctic Ocean. In 1792 he tried again, along the Peace River. After a five-week battle against its currents he reached its source high in the Rockies and crossed a ridge to a stream that flowed west. Boulder-strewn rapids made this river even more dangerous than the first. Local Native Americans warned him that no boat could navigate the terrible canyons there, so he and his men went west on foot. They forced a way through the forests and snow, and over yet more mountains, to a river that led them at last to the Pacific Ocean.

RAGING CURRENTS dashed Mackenzie's canoe onto rocks in a tributary of the treacherous river later named the Fraser. The crew was thrown overboard and most of the supplies were lost.

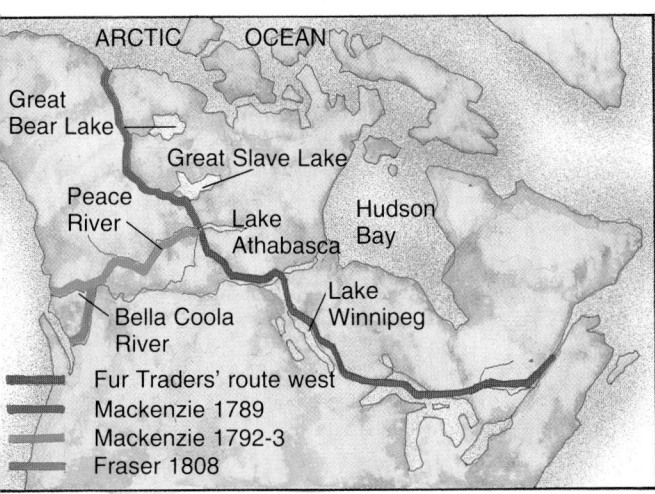

ARCTIC OCEAN

Great Bear Lake
Great Slave Lake
Peace River
Lake Athabasca
Hudson Bay
Bella Coola River
Lake Winnipeg

Fur Traders' route west
Mackenzie 1789
Mackenzie 1792-3
Fraser 1808

MACKENZIE reached the mouth of the Bella Coola River in British Columbia. He had set out from Montreal so he was the first to cross the continent (north of Mexico where Cabeza de Vaca had crossed) from coast to coast.

ON A ROCK near the Pacific he celebrated his achievement by writing in bold letters: "Alex Mackenzie from Canada by land 22nd July 1793". The letters (re-done in red concrete) are there today.

Mackenzie's canoe in the rapids.

THE TERRIBLE RIVER which Mackenzie had avoided was explored in 1808 by another fur trader, Simon Fraser. He followed it to the sea, but his expedition had to abandon its boats and follow the river-bank. The men had to cling to steep gorges that could only be crossed on Native American ladders of roots and bark, that swung in the wind.

Lewis and Clark

In 1718 the French got their Gulf colony going at last in New Orleans, but they could not find a profitable use for Louisiana and left most of it unexplored. During the 18th century it changed hands between France and Spain, and was French again when Napoleon sold it to the United States in 1804. Thomas Jefferson, the American president, was interested in the trading advantages his country would have if it could set up an easier route to the Pacific than the one Mackenzie had just found for the British. With this in mind he sent an official expedition west to explore America's new territory. It was led by two army officers: Meriwether Lewis and William Clark.

THE KEELBOAT, in which the expedition set off, was a traditional flat-bottomed, square-sailed riverboat. It made slow headway up the tumultous Missouri River. The crew had to strain on tow-ropes, sometimes through prickly undergrowth on the bank, sometimes up to their waists in water.

LEWIS (*LEFT*) AND CLARK were a well-balanced team. Lewis was the scholarly one interested in scientific exploration. He was also an excellent organizer, but quiet and aloof, too. His level-headed friend Clark was a friendly second-in-command.

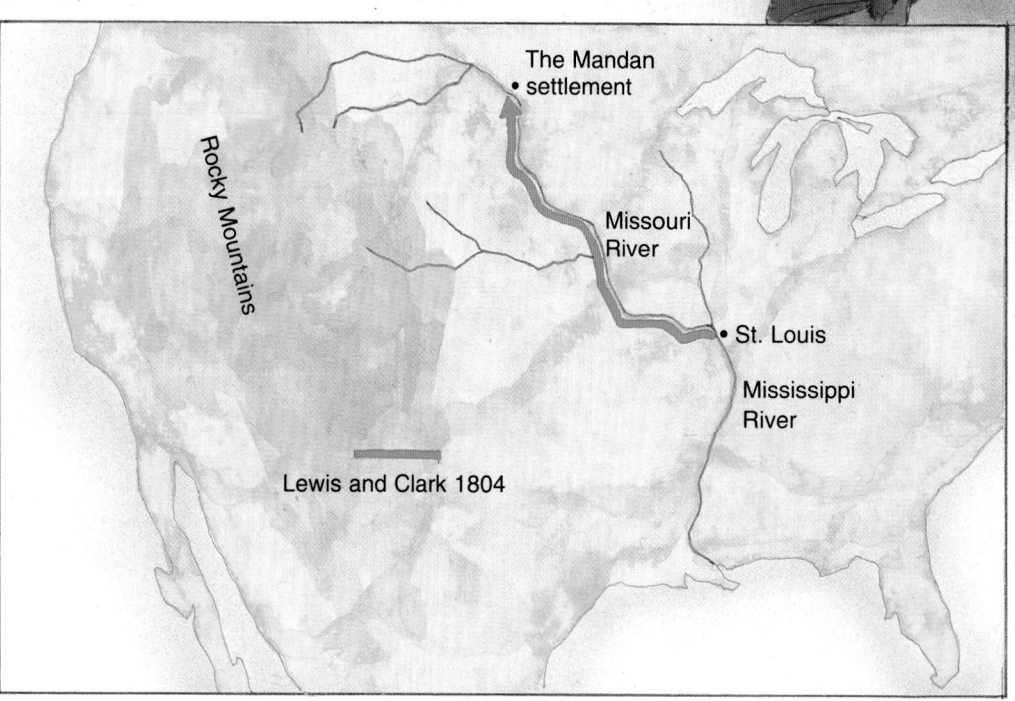

The Mandan settlement

Rocky Mountains

Missouri River

St. Louis

Mississippi River

Lewis and Clark 1804

THIS IS THE COMPASS that William Clark took with him. The purpose of the expedition was to make accurate observations so that maps could later be made. Scenery and events were recorded daily in notebooks. Clark illustrated his entries with many little sketches.

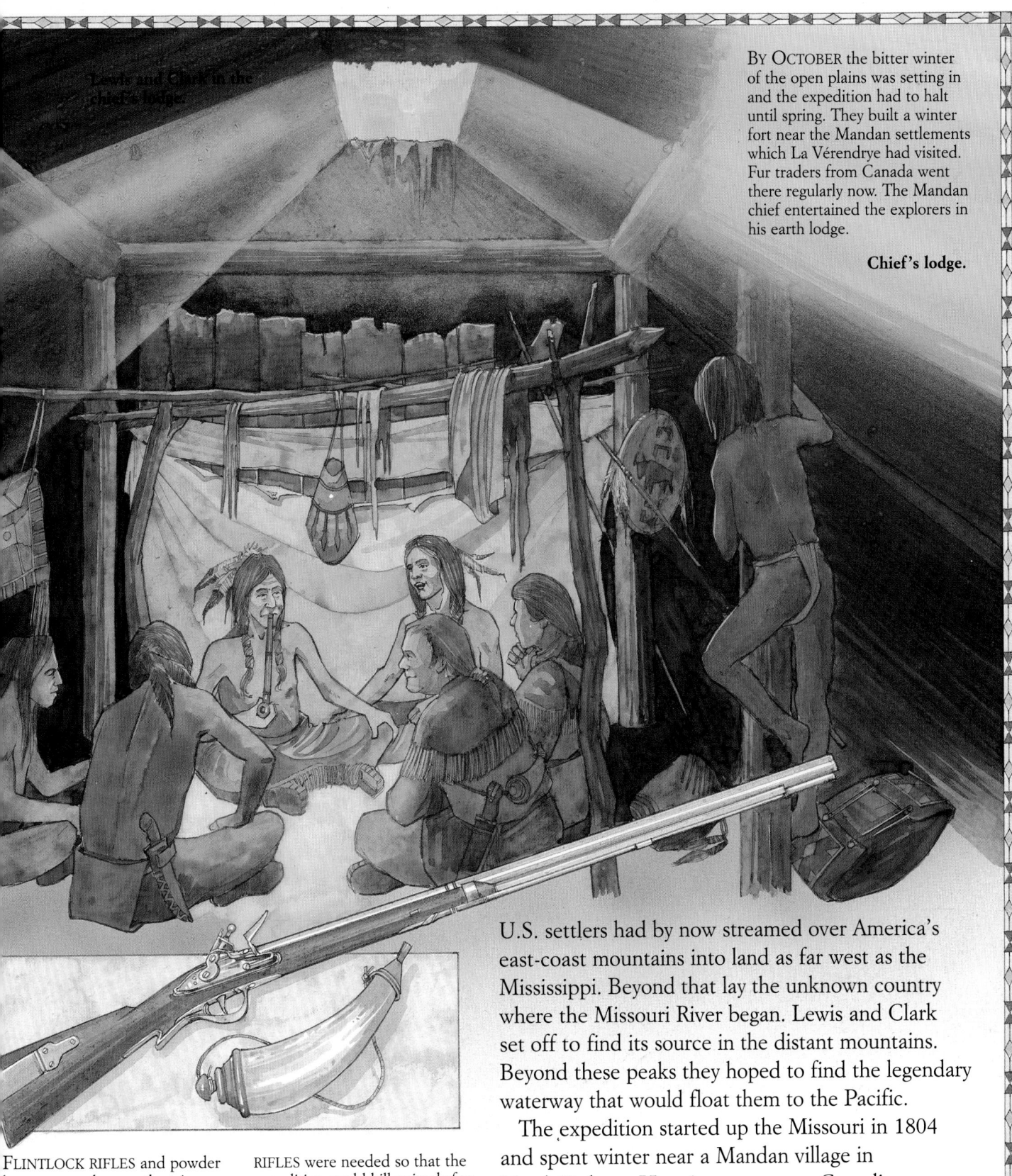

Lewis and Clark in the chief's lodge.

By OCTOBER the bitter winter of the open plains was setting in and the expedition had to halt until spring. They built a winter fort near the Mandan settlements which La Vérendrye had visited. Fur traders from Canada went there regularly now. The Mandan chief entertained the explorers in his earth lodge.

Chief's lodge.

FLINTLOCK RIFLES and powder horns were taken on the trip, but hardly anyone was shot at on the way.
Some native people, like the Sioux of the plains, were hostile because of past experiences with fur traders. Most local people the expedition met were friendly and helpful.

RIFLES were needed so that the expedition could kill animals for food. They were needed also as defense against the dangerous brown bears and grizzly bears that lived in the forest. Lewis was almost killed by a bear; he had forgotten the hunter's basic rule of never for an instant letting a rifle stay unloaded.

U.S. settlers had by now streamed over America's east-coast mountains into land as far west as the Mississippi. Beyond that lay the unknown country where the Missouri River began. Lewis and Clark set off to find its source in the distant mountains. Beyond these peaks they hoped to find the legendary waterway that would float them to the Pacific.

The expedition started up the Missouri in 1804 and spent winter near a Mandan village in North Dakota. Here it came across Canadian *coureurs de bois* (*see pages 22-3*) from the north. One of them had his young Shoshone-Indian wife, Sacajawea, with him. When Lewis and Clark decided to employ the husband on the expedition, Sacajawea, with a new-born baby, went too.

To the river of the West

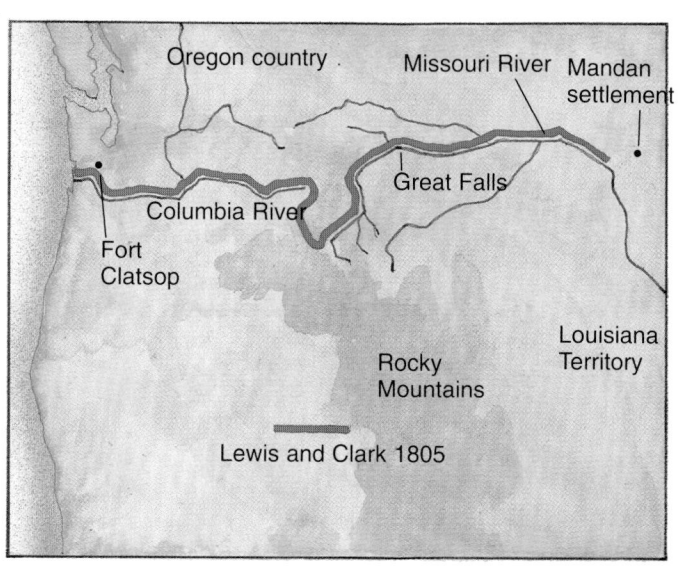

IN THE ROCKIES Sacajawea had a joyful surprise. She realized that she was back in the land of her people, the Shoshone, from whom she had been captured long ago. When the expedition met a party of Shoshones, she was asked to interpret.
At the sight of their chief she burst into tears of joy: he was her brother and she had never expected to see him again.

LIKE MACKENZIE who had crossed much farther north, Lewis and Clark reached the Rockies at a point where there was no easy way over.
The long journey down the western rivers took them only a quarter of the time they had spent in the mountains. The team built a fort on the Pacific and spent a rainy winter there before returning east.

Sacajawea recognizes her brother.

In April 1805 Lewis and Clark's team started up the unknown upper Missouri River. First they crossed the wide plains, sighting many herds of buffalo. On May 26 they saw the distant snowy summits of the Rockies. Further on, they spent a month getting around 17 miles of waterfalls. They had to make rough carts to haul the boats and gear past them.

The country grew wild and mountainous and the river became narrower and more hazardous.
By August the team were among the peaks where the river was a mountain stream too small for boats. The leaders were anxious; food was in short supply – there was little to hunt so high up – and they needed horses to get them over the Rockies before winter.

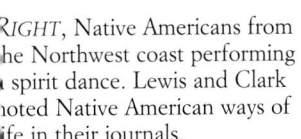

RIGHT, Native Americans from the Northwest coast performing a spirit dance. Lewis and Clark noted Native American ways of life in their journals.

BELOW, in November, near the mouth of the Columbia River, Lewis and Clark's party met a Chinook Indian chief. Sacajawea did not know the language but tried to communicate in signs.

The party meet a Chinook chief.

PEOPLE HAD KNOWN since 1792 that there was a great river to the west. American sea-trader Robert Gray had found the mouth of the river and named it the Columbia, after his ship.

Through a lucky meeting with Shoshone Indians, the expedition got pack-horses and crossed to the western slopes. The Shoshones warned that the nearest river fell through an impassable gorge, so the team trekked north along dizzying ridges to look for a better route. Horses fell down cliffs, the party was starving and snow fell.

Four months after entering the Rockies, the travelers came at last into a gentle river-valley. They made dug-out canoes and continued west, shooting rapids recklessly in their eagerness to find the western sea. On October 16 they entered a great river and knew that this must be the Columbia. It would sweep them to the sea – their mission had succeeded.

South Pass

Lewis and Clark's route was no use for ordinary travel. The credit for exploring the Rockies and finding a safe way over goes to some less distinguished but no less courageous explorers – the mountain men.

As Lewis and Clark were returning home through the eastern foothills of the Rockies, they were amazed to meet two rough-looking Americans, 1,500 miles from civilization: they were fur trappers. A few shrewd Americans had realized that these distant lands held as much of a fortune in furs as Canada. Within the next 20 years fur trapping became a way of life for Americans with a taste for adventure in the wilds. Many spent the whole year in the mountains, collecting beaver pelts. At an agreed time each year these "mountain men" went to a pre-arranged rendezvous in the Rockies (the spot varied from year to year), to sell their year's catch to the agents sent by fur companies.

The trappers found the Blackfoot Indians along the Missouri very hostile and were forced to look for more southerly routes into the mountains. In February 1824 a party of trappers led by mountain man Jedediah Smith were trying to reach trapping grounds on the western slopes when they found their usual route blocked by snow. A Crow Indian directed them further south. After a month spent retreating from blizzards they came upon a broad dip in the crest of the Rockies. This was South Pass, which became the gateway to the west.

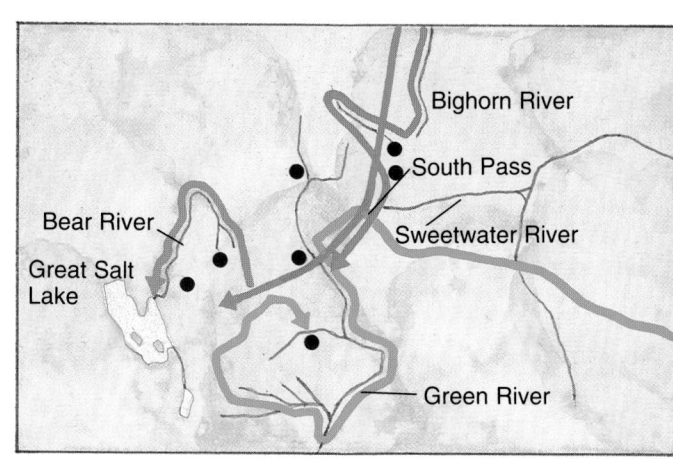

Bighorn River
South Pass
Bear River
Sweetwater River
Great Salt Lake
Green River

▬ Smith 1823
▬ Ashley 1824-5
▬ Henry's Party 1824
▬ Bridger 1825
● Rendezvous site

THESE MOUNTAIN MEN marked out the trails into the valleys of the western Rockies. After South Pass was discovered it became their regular route.

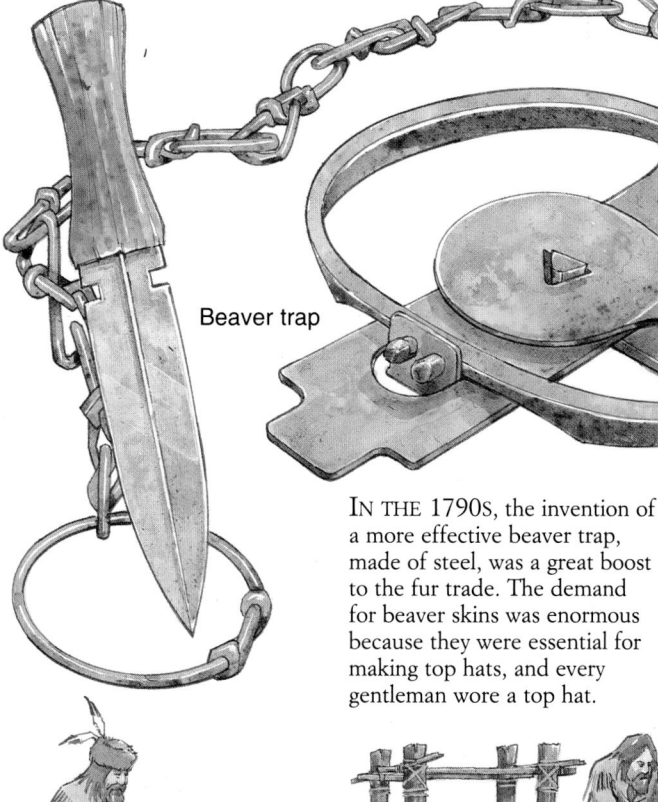

Beaver trap

IN THE 1790S, the invention of a more effective beaver trap, made of steel, was a great boost to the fur trade. The demand for beaver skins was enormous because they were essential for making top hats, and every gentleman wore a top hat.

BEAVERS are riverbank animals that spend much of their time in the water. The trapper put the baited trap underwater and anchored it to a stake.

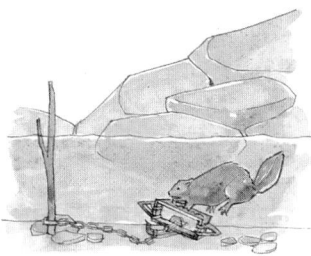

WHEN A BEAVER touched the bait-pan in the center of the trap, the spring was released and the beaver was trapped underwater by its paw.

THE TRAPPER cleaned each beaver pelt by scraping its underside with a metal scraper. This was done on a sloping graining block.

THE PELTS were pressed to flatten them and then they were made up into bales of a standard weight for transport to the rendezvous.

THE RENDEZVOUS was like a huge fair held in the wilderness. The arrival of the fur companies' mule trains, laden with supplies, was the signal for the start of the festivities. The trappers were paid for their furs, and there was plenty of food and whiskey.

THE WEATHERBEATEN mountain men dressed in buckskins like the Native Americans. Some had Native American wives. They all made the most of the occasion singing, dancing and often brawling, until late at night.

SIOUX INDIANS from the Plains and Shoshones from west of the Rockies came to the gatherings and put up their tepees. They sold horses and buffalo-skin robes in exchange for guns and knives. They joined in the feasting and drinking, too.

MANY MOUNTAIN MEN spent all their money immediately on drinking and gambling. After buying ammunition and supplies for the coming year what was the point of saving the rest? They could not spend it in the mountains.

A rendezvous.

To California

Mountain men continued to explore beyond the Rockies in search of furs. They discovered the Great Salt Lake and the best way northwest towards the Columbia River from South Pass. The mountain man with the biggest reputation for discovery was Jedediah Smith. He was a record-breaking trapper with such a knowledge of the wilds that his party would follow him anywhere. He survived a Native American massacre and had been mauled by a grizzly (but he got a companion to stitch his ear back on). He was a sober, religious man who took his bible everywhere. Unlike most mountain men who thought mainly of making profit, he was led by the thrill of exploration.

In August 1826 Smith went southwest from the Great Salt Lake with 15 men, to find beaver. No white person had gone that way before. The hunt turned into a struggle for survival as they crossed the bare dry region between the Rockies and the Sierra Nevada. Geographers later named this area the Great Basin. After nine weeks of following rivers that were mostly dry, the party was starving. They were on foot as their horses were too weak to carry them, but they managed to reach a village of Mojave Indians. There was a tense moment as the Mojaves put spears to the travelers' throats but Smith offered gifts to show they were friends. The Mojaves helped them recover and told them that a lush valley, California (a Mexican colony), lay just over the mountains to the west – across a terrible desert.

The Mojave Desert.

40

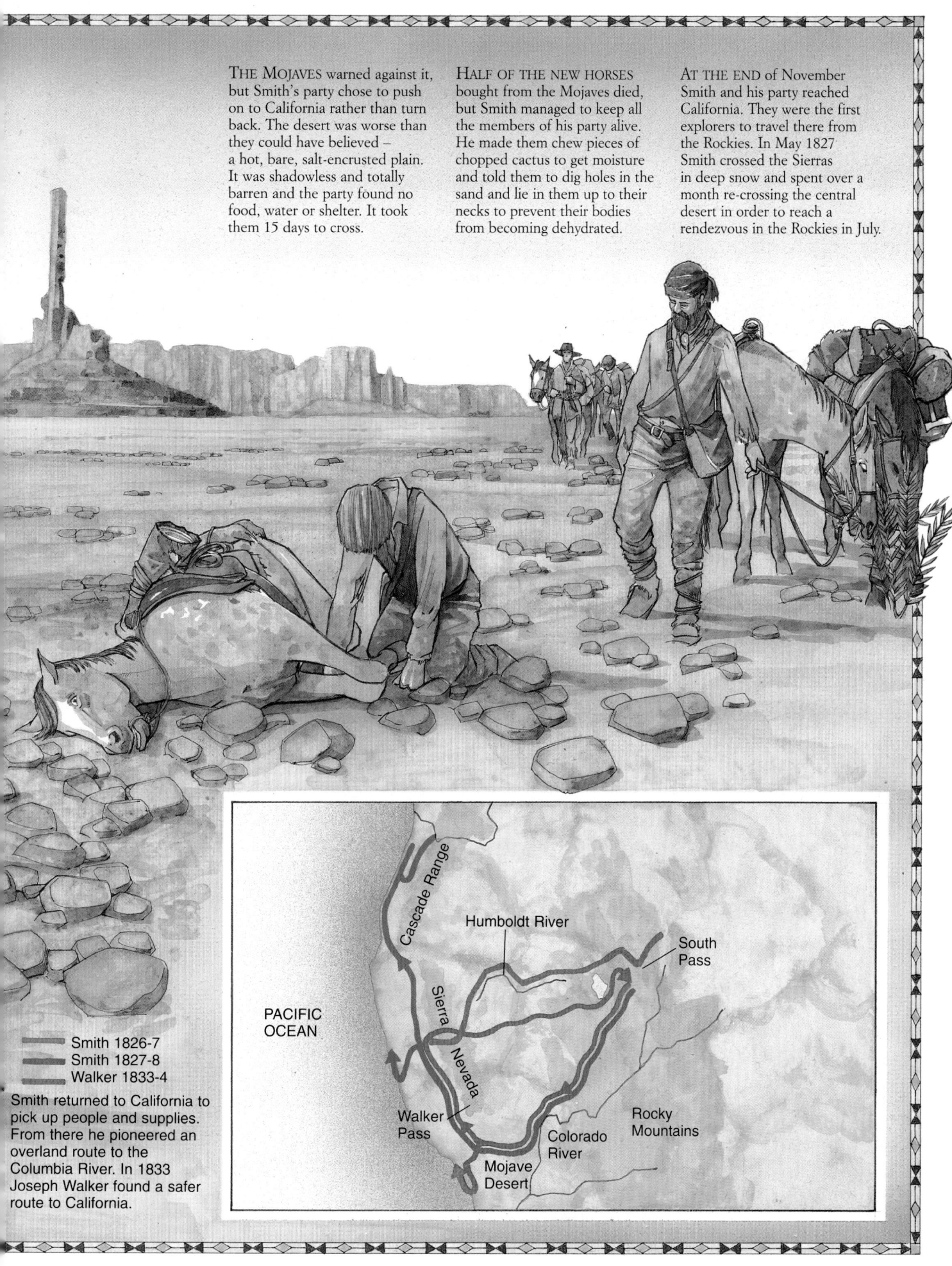

THE MOJAVES warned against it, but Smith's party chose to push on to California rather than turn back. The desert was worse than they could have believed – a hot, bare, salt-encrusted plain. It was shadowless and totally barren and the party found no food, water or shelter. It took them 15 days to cross.

HALF OF THE NEW HORSES bought from the Mojaves died, but Smith managed to keep all the members of his party alive. He made them chew pieces of chopped cactus to get moisture and told them to dig holes in the sand and lie in them up to their necks to prevent their bodies from becoming dehydrated.

AT THE END of November Smith and his party reached California. They were the first explorers to travel there from the Rockies. In May 1827 Smith crossed the Sierras in deep snow and spent over a month re-crossing the central desert in order to reach a rendezvous in the Rockies in July.

Smith 1826-7
Smith 1827-8
Walker 1833-4

Smith returned to California to pick up people and supplies. From there he pioneered an overland route to the Columbia River. In 1833 Joseph Walker found a safer route to California.

Cascade Range

Humboldt River

South Pass

PACIFIC OCEAN

Sierra Nevada

Walker Pass

Rocky Mountains

Colorado River

Mojave Desert

The Way West

The discovery of South Pass – the only easy way across the Rockies – changed the way that the people of the United States thought about the American continent and their place in it. Until then the far west had seemed too remote for most of them to bother with. Then in the 1830s word got around that the Pacific regions – Oregon (the Columbia area to which Britain had a claim) and California (belonging to Mexico) – were lands of opportunity where fortunes could be made. South Pass was the gateway to these lands. Many U.S. citizens were suddenly in a hurry to settle there. They believed it was their nation's destiny to fill the continent from coast to coast with American citizens.

By the early 1840s pioneering families were making the difficult five-month journey over the South Pass and on to the Pacific. Some had mountain men to guide them but there was an urgent need for routes to be mapped properly. In 1842 the U.S. government gave this task to army surveyor, Captain John Charles Frémont. Frémont was a great self-publicist. He made the reports of his expeditions west into such exciting reading that they sold in vast numbers and helped to boost enthusiasm for moving west. He became known as the Great Pathfinder, though much of what he mapped had already been found. But he has discoveries to his credit. He was the first to explain the rivers of the Great Basin (they never reach the sea) and deserves to be recognized as the last of the great explorers of North America.

IN 1842 Frémont mapped the first half of the Oregon Trail – the most practical route west. This followed the Platte River, which was too shallow for boats, towards South Pass. He then explored the Wind River range.

IN 1843-4 Frémont explored the Great Salt Lake and the rest of the Trail. Then he went south from Oregon along the west side of the Great Basin to see whether any river cut through the Sierra Nevada to the sea.

PIONEERS TREKKED more than 2,000 miles, from the Missouri to the Pacific, in covered wagons. The way to the west, which explorers had sought for so long, proved not to be a great waterway after all, but a long hard overland trail.

FRÉMONT discovered lakes on the way, including Pyramid Lake (*below*), but the river he was searching for did not exist. He had to make a dangerous winter crossing of the Sierra to reach California.

Frémont 1842
Frémont 1843-4
Frémont 1845
Frémont 1848-9

Sierra Nevada

Great Basin

Great Salt Lake

Frémont Peak

Missouri River

South Pass

Frémont's party at Pyramid Lake.

IN 1842 Frémont climbed what he thought was the highest peak in the Rockies and planted the American flag on top.

43

TIME CHART

1492 — Columbus discovers Hispaniola.

1497 — Cabot becomes the first European since the Vikings to visit Newfoundland.

1498 — On his third voyage, Columbus lands on the South American mainland, in the delta of the Orinoco River.

1513 — Ponce de León lands in Florida.

1519-21 — Cortés travels from Cuba to Mexico in search of gold.

1524 — Verrazano explores the Atlantic coast from North Carolina to Newfoundland.

1528 — Narváez lands in Florida and travels inland.

c. 1529-36 — Cabeza de Vaca, Esteban and two others wander through Texas, New Mexico and along the Gulf of California.

1534 — Cartier sails to the east coast of Newfoundland and explores the Gulf of Saint Lawrence.

1535-6 — Cartier explores the Saint Lawrence River.

1539 — Father Marcos and Esteban travel into Arizona.

1539-42 — de Soto explores a large area of south-eastern America crossing the Mississippi.

1542 — Death of de Soto. His expedition is brought home by Moscoso.

1540-42 — Coronado travels through Arizona, Texas, Oklahoma and Kansas. A party of his men see the Grand Canyon.

1576 — Frobisher reaches Baffin Island.

1604-7 — Champlain explores and maps out the coast of Nova Scotia.

1606 — Hudson explores the mouth of the Hudson River.

1608 — Champlain founds Quebec.

1609-16 — Champlain travels from the Saint Lawrence River to Lake Champlain, and later to Lake Huron and Lake Ontario.

1610   Hudson discovers Hudson Bay.

1621   Brûlé sees Lake Superior.

1634-5 Nicolet travels from Lake Huron to Lake Michigan and learns of the existence of the Mississippi River.

1665-7 Father Allouez travels to Lake Nipigon.

1673   Joliet and Father Marquette descend the Mississippi.

1680   Father Hennepin discovers Saint Anthony's Falls.

1682   La Salle descends the Mississippi River to the Gulf of Mexico.

1731-6 La Vérendrye explores northwest from Lake Superior to Lake Winnipeg.

1738   La Vérendrye and his sons travel through North Dakota to the Missouri River.

1742   La Vérendrye's sons explore southwest of the Missouri and see distant mountain ranges.

1778   Captain Cook, searching for the Pacific end of the northwest passage, sails into Nootka Sound on the west coast of Vancouver Island.

1789   Mackenzie discovers the Mackenzie River and follows it to the Arctic Ocean.

1792   Gray sails into the mouth of the Columbia River.

1793   Mackenzie reaches the Pacific coast overland, at the mouth of the Bella Coola River.

1804   President Jefferson sends Lewis and Clark to find an American route to the Pacific.

1805   Lewis and Clark set off into unknown territory in April. They reach the Pacific in November.

1808   Fraser descends the Fraser River to the Pacific.

1824   Jedediah Smith discovers South Pass.

1826   Smith is the first to reach California overland from the Rockies.

1833   Joseph Walker pioneers a safer route to California, avoiding much of the desert by following the Humboldt River. His route later becomes the "California Trail".

1842   Frémont begins his survey of the Oregon Trail.

1843-4 Frémont completes his survey of the trail, explores the western side of the Great Basin and is the first to cross the Sierras in winter.

1845   Frémont's continued search for the best way across the Sierras is interrupted by war between the U.S. and Mexico, in which the Americans gain California.

1848-9 Frémont attempts a mid-winter survey of a possible rail route through the mountains but, after terrible hardships, is forced back by the weather.

GLOSSARY

Algonquin
a Native American tribe of eastern Canada.

Blackfeet
Plains Indian peoples whose homelands were in Montana and neighboring Canada.

Buffalo
(so-called, but correct term is bison; true buffalo live in Asia and Africa) very large wild cattle, found in vast herds on the North American plains before white settlers shot most of them.

Canyon
a deep, steep-sided river-gorge.

Chinook
salmon-fishing and hunting tribe of the Pacific coast, near the mouth of the Columbia River.

Conquistadores
military commanders sent by Spain to explore and conquer land in the New World.

El Dorado
legendary ruler of a land fabulously rich in gold. In the 16th and 17th centuries, the land was thought to exist in the New World.

Estuary
the mouth of a river, where tidal waters enter from the sea.

Flintlock rifle
a rifle with a firing mechanism which uses a flint to strike sparks to ignite gunpowder.

Fountain of Youth
legendary wonder supposed to exist somewhere in the New World. Anyone who bathed in it would remain young forever.

Great Basin
geographical term for a large, semi-desert area of western North America, between the Rockies and the Sierra Nevada.

Gunwale
upper edge of a boat's sides.

Hurons
village-dwelling farmers and hunters of the Great Lakes region. They were driven from their homelands by the Iroquois in the 17th century.

Isthmus
a narrow strip of land, with water on either side, connecting two larger areas of land.

Landfall
a landing point that end a long sea voyage.

Latitude
the distance north or south of the equator, of any point on the globe. The latitude of a particular point can be discovered by observing from it the apparent height above the horizon of the sun or particular stars. This enabled travelers at sea, or in unknown surroundings, to know how far north or south they had reached.

Longitude
a measurement of distance east or west of an imaginary north-south line from pole to pole. Longitude cannot be measured by observing the sun or stars. Until delicate timekeeping instruments were perfected in the 18th century, explorers had to make a rough calculation of how far they had moved east or west of their starting point. They calculated the time their journey had taken, the direction they traveled and their probable overall speed.

Mandans
Plains Indians of the upper Missouri River. Unlike most Plains Indians they lived in villages and farmed, as well as hunted buffalo.

Mangrove
a tropical tree that grows on swampy coasts. It sends a tangle of above-water roots down into the mud.

Matchlock musket
a 16th-century hand-gun in which the powder was ignited by a match.

Mojave
a farming, fishing and hunting people of the lower Colorado River.

Mutiny
to refuse to obey the orders of someone lawfully in command.

Plains Indians
a number of different nomadic tribes of the central plains of North America, who depended on the buffalo for all their needs.

Powder Horn
an ox- or cow-horn made into a container for gunpowder. Its shape was ideal for pouring a small amount of powder into the gun.

Punt
to propel a boat by thrusting against the river-bed with a long pole.

Quadrant
an instrument for measuring latitude.

Sandspit a strip of land created when tides continually deposit sand in a line parallel with the coast, or across the mouth of a bay.

Seven Golden Cities of Cibola
fabled cities of a legendary New World land.

Shoshone
a number of related tribes of differing lifestyles, who lived mostly west of the Rockies, from southwest Montana to eastern California.

Sioux
a large group of Plains Indian tribes, which include the Blackfeet. The Sioux were outstanding warriors.

Strait
a narrow sea-passage between larger areas of the sea.

Winnebagoes
a farming people of eastern Wisconsin.

Yaqui
an agricultural tribe living along the Yaqui River in Mexico, and in Arizona.

Zuñi
one of the Pueblo peoples of Arizona and New Mexico. They built mud-brick villages of multi-story houses.

INDEX